Blueprints Q&A
STEP 3: SURGERY

Blueprints Q&A
STEP 3: SURGERY

SERIES EDITOR:
Michael S. Clement, MD

Fellow, American Academy of Pediatrics
Mountain Park Health Center
Phoenix, Arizona
Clinical Lecturer in Family
 and Community Medicine
University of Arizona College of Medicine
Consultant, Arizona Department
 of Health Services

EDITOR:
Edward W. Nelson, MD

Professor of Surgery
University of Utah
Attending Surgeon
University of Utah Medical Center
Salt Lake City, Utah

**Blackwell
Science**

EDITORIAL OFFICES:

Commerce Place, 350 Main Street,
    Malden, Massachusetts 02148, USA

Osney Mead, Oxford OX2 0EL, England

25 John Street, London WC1N 2BS, England

23 Ainslie Place, Edinburgh EH3 6AJ, Scotland

54 University Street, Carlton, Victoria 3053, Australia

OTHER EDITORIAL OFFICES:

Blackwell Wissenschafts-Verlag GmbH,
    Kurfürstendamm 57, 10707 Berlin, Germany

Blackwell Science KK, MG Kodenmacho Building,
    7-10 Kodenmacho Nihombashi, Chuo-ku,
    Tokyo 104, Japan

Iowa State University Press, A Blackwell Science Company,
    2121 S. State Avenue, Ames, Iowa 50014-8300, USA

DISTRIBUTORS:

The Americas
Blackwell Publishing
c/o AIDC
P.O. Box 20
50 Winter Sport Lane
Williston, VT 05495-0020
(Telephone orders: 800-216-2522;
fax orders: 802-864-7626)

Australia Blackwell Science Pty, Ltd.
54 University Street
Carlton, Victoria 3053
(Telephone orders: 03-9347-0300;
fax orders: 03-9349-3016)

Outside The Americas and Australia
Blackwell Science, Ltd.
c/o Marston Book Services, Ltd., P.O. Box 269
Abingdon, Oxon OX14 4YN, England
(Telephone orders: 44-01235-465500;
fax orders: 44-01235-465555)

Acquisitions: Beverly Copland

Development: Julia Casson

Production: Elissa Gershowitz

Manufacturing: Lisa Flanagan

Marketing Manager: Toni Fournier

Cover design by Hannus Design

Typeset by International Typesetting and Composition

Printed and bound by Courier-Stoughton

Printed in the United States of America

01 02 03 04 5 4 3 2 1

The Blackwell Science logo is a trade mark of Blackwell
Science Ltd., registered at the United Kingdom Trade Marks
Registry

Library of Congress Cataloging-in-Publication Data

Blueprints Q & A step 3. Surgery / editor,
Edward W. Nelson.
        p. ; cm.—(Blueprints Q & A step 3 series)
    ISBN 0-632-04616-0 (pbk.)
    1. Surgery—Examinations, questions, etc.
    2. Physicians—Licenses—United States—Examinations—
        Study guides.
    [DNLM: 1. Surgery—Examination Questions. 2. Surgical
Procedures, Operative—Examination Questions.
WO 18.2 B6582 2002] I. Title: Blueprints Q & A step 3. Surgery.
II. Title: Blueprints Q and A step three. Surgery. III. Title:
Surgery. IV. Nelson, Edward W. V. Series.
    RD37.2 .B582 2002
    617′.0076—dc21   2001006340

Notice: The indications and dosages of all drugs in this book
have been recommended in the medical literature and con-
form to the practices of the general community. The medications described and treatment prescriptions suggested
do not necessarily have specific approval by the Food and
Drug Administration for use in the diseases and dosages for
which they are recommended. The package insert for each
drug should be consulted for use and dosage as approved
by the FDA. Because standards for usage change, it is advisable to keep abreast of revised recommendations, particularly those concerning new drugs.

CONTRIBUTORS

Stephen H. Bailey, MD
Resident, General Surgery
University of Utah
Salt Lake City, Utah

Michelle T. Mueller, MD
Resident, General Surgery
University of Utah
Salt Lake City, Utah

Clinton B. Webster, MD
Resident, General Surgery
University of Utah
Salt Lake City, Utah

REVIEWERS

William R. Wrightson, M.D.
Resident in Surgery
University of Louisville
Louisville, Kentucky

Aaron B. Caughey MD, MPP, MPH
Fellow, Maternal-Fetal Medicine
Department of Obstetrics and Gynecology
University of California, San Francisco
San Francisco, California

Patrick G. Dean, MD
Resident, Department of General Surgery
Mayo Clinic and Foundation
Rochester, Minnesota

PREFACE

The *Blueprints* Q&A Step 3 series has been developed to complement our core content *Blueprints* books. Each *Blueprints* Q&A Step 3 book (*Medicine, Pediatrics, Surgery, Psychiatry,* and *Obstetrics/ Gynecology*) was written by residents seeking to provide the highest quality of practice review questions simulating the USMLE.

Like the actual USMLE Step 3 exam, this book is divided into different practice settings: Community-Based Health Center, Office, In-Patient Facility, and Emergency Department. Each book covers a single discipline, allowing you to use them during "down-time." Each book contains 100 review cases that cover content typical to the Step 3 USMLE.

Answers are found at the end of each setting, with the correct option highlighted. Accompanying the correct answer is a discussion of why the other options are incorrect. This allows for even the wrong answers to provide you with a valuable learning experience.

Blackwell has been fortunate to work with expert editors and residents—people like you who have studied for and passed the Boards. They sought to provide you with the very best practice prior to taking the Boards.

We welcome feedback and suggestions you may have about this book or any in the *Blueprints* series. Send to blue@blacksci.com.

All of the authors and staff at Blackwell wish you well on the Boards, and in your medical future!

BLOCK **ONE**

QUESTIONS

Setting I: Community-Based Health Center

This is a community-based health facility where patients seeking both routine and urgent care are encountered. Many patients are low income; many are ethnic minorities. Several industrial parks and local small businesses send employees there with on-the-job injuries and for employee health screening. There is capability for x-ray films, but CT and MRI must be arranged at other facilities. Laboratory services are available.

QUESTION 1

A 55-year-old, otherwise healthy, man is 30 months status post right hemicolectomy for a T2N1M0 carcinoma of the colon. He received 5-FU and leucovorin postoperatively. Some mild abdominal pain prompted a CT scan that revealed a 1.5-cm single lesion, consistent with a metastasis, in the left lateral segment of the liver. Appropriate therapy at this time is:

A. Exploratory laparotomy and left lateral segmentectomy

B. Repeat administration of 5-FU/leucovorin

C. Local radiation therapy

D. No further therapy

QUESTION 2

A 32-year-old healthy Caucasian woman presents to you with 1-month history of abdominal pain. She is G0P0, has had no prior hospitalizations or surgeries, has no allergies, and takes only oral contraceptive pills. You obtain an abdominal ultrasound suspecting symptomatic cholelithiasis, but no stones are found. (See Figure 2.) However, a 5-cm mass is noted at the periphery of the right lobe of the liver. The most common benign cause of this lesion is:

A. Focal nodular hyperplasia

B. Hepatic adenoma

C. Hemangioma

D. Hamartoma

E. None of the above

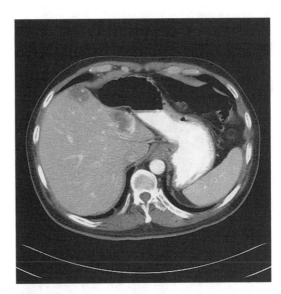

FIGURE 2

QUESTION 3

Multiple diagnostic studies suggest that this woman's lesion is a hepatic adenoma. (See Figure 3.) Which one or more of the following is/are true with regard to hepatic adenoma?

A. The first step in managing this problem is to stop oral contraceptives.

B. Hepatic adenoma has the potential for malignant degeneration.

C. Hepatic adenoma has a risk of spontaneous rupture.

D. Hepatic adenoma has a risk of spontaneous bleeding.

E. All of the above are true.

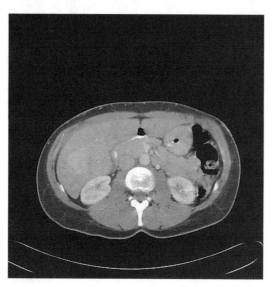

FIGURE 3

QUESTION 4

A 68-year-old man presents to you with a complaint of intermittent, painless blood in his urine. The first diagnostic test that you should order is:

A. Cystography

B. Intravenous pyelogram (IVP)

C. Intravenous urogram

D. Plain abdominal film

E. Urinalysis

QUESTION 5

The above patient has a normal CBC, and Chem 7. Urinalysis reveals microscopic hematuria. Intravenous pyelogram and urogram are without abnormality. Cystography reveals a 2-cm area that appears to be transitional cell cancer of the bladder. What is the next step in dealing with this problem?

A. Resection of the lesion through the cystoscope

B. Intravesicular BCG

C. Intravesicular thiotepa

D. Biopsy of the lesion through the cystoscope

E. None of the above

QUESTION 6

You see a 36-year-old woman in the clinic. She has a 2-cm pigmented lesion on her left arm, which has been present for 3 years but recently increased in size. The most appropriate next step is:

A. Take a picture and reevaluate in 6 weeks

B. Shave biopsy

C. Excisional biopsy

D. Partial excisional biopsy

E. None of the above

QUESTION 7

A 68-year-old male smoker presents to you with a chronic cough. CXR reveals a 2-cm mass in the right upper lobe that was not present on an x-ray taken one year earlier. The most appropriate next step in working up this nodule is:

A. Chest CT scan

B. Chest ultrasound

C. Thoracoscopy

D. Mediastinoscopy

E. Fine needle aspiration for cytologic diagnosis

QUESTION 8

The above patient has the following preoperative studies. Which study provides an absolute contraindication to undergoing a surgical right upper lobectomy?

A. $FEV1 < 0.8$ L

B. $PaO_2 < 50$ Torr

C. $PaCO_2 > 50$ Torr

D. Vital capacity < 1.5 L

E. None of the above

QUESTION 9

A 46-year-old female diabetic presents to your office with an unintended 65-lb weight loss over 8 months. You notice a raised, red, pruritic rash with erythema and scaling on the patient's pretibial, perioral, and intertriginous areas. The patient states that she has had this rash for years despite multiple treatment regimens from her dermatologist. You quickly discover the other physician's errors and confirm your diagnosis by obtaining:

A. Dexamethasone suppression test

B. Serum glucagon level

C. C-peptide/insulin ratio

D. Neurotensin level

E. PTH

QUESTION 10

The second most common location of this type of abdominal tumor causing hyperacidity is:

A. Duodenum

B. Small bowel mesentery

C. Liver

D. Retroperitoneum

E. Stomach

QUESTION 11

After successful surgical management by enucleation with clear margins and no evidence of metastases, the above patient inquires about her risk for recurrence. You tell her:

A. Most patients are cured with surgical resection.

B. The overall 5-year survival is about 50%.

C. These tumors are fast growing and micrometastases will appear quickly if present.

D. Most tumors of this type are not malignant.

E. There is no additional therapy available.

QUESTION 12

Your patient is a 30-year-old woman with a history of easy bruising, mucosal bleeding, and petechiae. On examination you note multiple areas of ecchymosis and petechiae. A CBC reveals a WBC of 8000, Hct of 39, and platelets of 30,000. The most appropriate next step in management is:

A. Intravenous immune globulin

B. Prednisone, 1 mg/kg/day

C. Emergent splenectomy

D. Technetium 99-m colloid liver spleen scan

E. Infusion of a 6-pack of platelets

QUESTION 13

You see a 4-year-old in the community health center with easy bruising and mucosal bleeding. His mother is very concerned since this started after a recent episode of the flu. The only abnormality on physical exam are multiple ecchymoses. Labs are normal with the exception of a platelet count of 40,000. You recommend to his mother:

A. Infusion of platelets as soon as possible

B. Strict bed rest with avoidance of contact sports

C. Counseling for child abuse

D. Splenectomy

E. A course of prednisone

QUESTION 14

You see a 37-year-old, otherwise healthy, woman who complains of abdominal pain. On further questioning she reveals increased abdominal girth with a marked increase in her waist size over the last couple of months. On examination you note a full abdomen with a fluid wave, hepatomegaly, and tenderness in the right upper quadrant. Labs reveal a normal liver panel, normal CBC, and a low albumin. An ultrasound confirms ascites, and a paracentesis reveals >3 g protein per deciliter. The most likely diagnosis is:

A. Alcoholic cirrhosis

B. Hepatitis C

C. Budd–Chiari syndrome

D. Gallbladder cancer

E. Splenic vein thrombosis

QUESTION 15

Possible appropriate surgical interventions for the above patient include all of the following EXCEPT:

A. Portasystemic decompression

B. Liver transplantation

C. Cholecystectomy

D. Peritoneovenous shunt

E. Venous thrombectomy

QUESTION 16

A 5-week-old, breast fed, term, boy presents to you with a 3-day history of fussiness and vomiting. The boy's vomiting has become projectile in nature over the past day but it is nonbilious. He is now unable to keep down breast milk. He exhibits tenting skin and a sunken anterior fontanelle and has not had a wet diaper for 12 hr. The most likely diagnosis is:

A. Duodenal web

B. Hypertrophic pyloric stenosis

C. Annular pancreas

D. Midgut volvulus

E. Intestinal atresia

QUESTION 17

You admit the above patient to the hospital and are appropriately concerned about electrolyte and fluid imbalances. The most likely electrolyte status in this patient is:

A. Hyperkalemic, hyperchloremic metabolic alkalosis

B. Hypokalemic, hypochloremic metabolic alkalosis

C. Hypokalemic, hyperchloremic metabolic alkalosis

D. Hyperkalemic, hypochloremic metabolic alkalosis

E. None of the above

QUESTION 18

After correction of fluid and electrolyte imbalances the appropriate therapy for this patient's problem is:

A. Gastrojejunostomy

B. IV fluids and antispasmodics

C. Pyloromyotomy

D. Lateral duodenotomy

E. Duodenojejunostomy

QUESTION 19

A 68-year-old man presents to your clinic complaining of chronic abdominal pain. He has had intermittent pain for the last several months and the pain is worse after meals. His wife states that this is impossible because he "never eats." He describes the pain as crampy and diffuse. Past medical history is notable for hypertension and coronary artery disease. He is 3 years status post a left femoral artery-popliteal artery bypass for claudication. Review of systems is notable for a recent unintended 10-lb weight loss, but no night sweats or bloody stool. The most likely diagnosis in this patient is:

A. Mesenteric ischemia

B. Gastrointestinal tumor

C. Gastroenteritis

D. Crohn's disease

E. Celiac sprue

QUESTION 20

The most appropriate next test to confirm the above diagnosis is:

A. CT scan

B. Abdominal films

C. Mesenteric angiogram

D. Upper endoscopy

E. Colonoscopy

QUESTION 21

Which of the following are potential mechanisms of acute mesenteric ischemia? (See Figure 21.)

A. Arterial thrombosis

B. Arterial embolus

C. Venous thrombosis

D. Non-occlusive mesenteric ischemia

E. All of the above are mechanisms of mesenteric ischemia

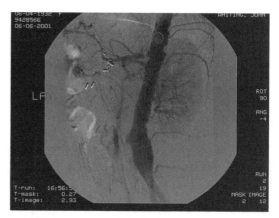

FIGURE 21

QUESTION 22

A 60-year-old comes to the health center complaining of abdominal pain. She is otherwise healthy and has no history of abdominal surgeries. On further questioning she tells you that this intermittent pain is localized to the umbilical region. On examination you note that she has an easily reducible mass at the umbilicus. You recommend surgical repair and she asks you if there is any way to avoid surgery. Your explanation includes which of the following points:

A. Almost all hernias should be surgically repaired.

B. Intestinal obstruction associated with hernias is a significant cause of morbidity and is preventable by surgical repair.

C. Umbilical hernias in children under 4 years old may be observed.

D. Some adults with overwhelming comorbidities may be observed.

E. All of the above.

QUESTION 23

A 70-year-old male comes to your office complaining of urinary hesitancy, poor urinary stream, and the need to get up to urinate at least six times a night. You are worried about BPH. Your next steps include all of the following EXCEPT:

A. Urinalysis with culture

B. CT scan

C. Ultrasound

D. Digital rectal exam

QUESTION 24

The above patient is found to have a UTI that you treat. You feel this is secondary to BPH. You check a PSA and treat his BPH with an alpha-antagonist and a 5-alpha-reductase inhibitor. He follows up with you and continues to complain of nocturia that has not improved since his last visit. The next step is:

A. Nothing, just continue the medication

B. Prostatectomy

C. Transurethral resection of the prostate

D. Repeat urinalysis with culture

QUESTION 25

A 12-year-old male is sent to your clinic from his new pediatrician's office for evaluation of left cryptorchidism. On examination you cannot palpate a left testicle. You recommend which of the following options to the patient and his parents:

A. Wait a few years to see if the testicle descends

B. Surgical exploration and scrotal placement of the testicle

C. Orchiectomy

D. CT scan to look for the testicle

E. Nothing, he has a normal right testicle

QUESTION 26

A 35-year-old male comes to see you complaining of a right testicular mass that his primary care physician noted on exam last week. The patient has no complaints of pain or UTI symptoms. On exam you rule out a hernia and identify the right testicular mass. The mass is firm, nontender, and is approximately 2-cm in size. You are concerned about a malignancy. Your next step includes all of the following EXCEPT:

A. Serum alpha-fetoprotein

B. Beta-human chorionic gonadotropin

C. Biopsy for tissue diagnosis

D. Wait and reexamine in 1 month

QUESTION 27

A 60-year-old male presents to the health center complaining of hematuria. He is otherwise fairly healthy with no past surgical history. He does take a beta-blocker and an aspirin for a small MI 5 years ago. He has no history of angina since the MI. He was a smoker but has not smoked for the last 5 years. Abdominal exam is benign and there are no hernias present. Urinalysis reveals the presence of RBCs, but no WBCs. CT scan is shown below (see Figure 27). You explain to him the treatment of choice is:

A. Wait and reevaluate by CT in 3 months

B. Further workup with IVP

C. Biopsy of the kidney

D. Radical nephrectomy

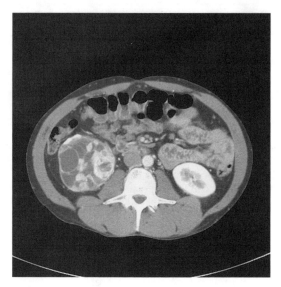

FIGURE 27

QUESTION 28

A 35-year-old male presents to your clinic with a 3-year history of intermittent abdominal pain, diarrhea, and a recent 40-lb weight loss. On review of symptoms, he has joint pain, occasional bouts of eye inflammation, and chronic chancre sores. You note on his social history that he is adopted with no contact with his biological family. On exam, he has obvious signs of malnutrition. This patient has a number of potential diagnoses, but your first priority should be to rule out:

A. Gastritis

B. Crohn's disease

C. Colon cancer

D. Gastroenteritis

E. Cholecystitis

QUESTION 29

You perform colonoscopy on the above patient. You see segments of inflamed colon interspersed with areas of normal appearing colon. The terminal ileum appears inflamed as well. Biopsies of the diseased segments will most likely show:

A. Granulomas

B. Pseudopolyps

C. Crypt abscesses

D. Isolated mucosal metaplasia

E. Increased mucus secretion

QUESTION 30

Laboratory test(s) for the above patient that will confirm the diagnosis is/are:

A. CEA

B. CA-19-9

C. AFP

D. PSA

E. None of the above

QUESTION 31

Drug therapy for this patient's disease can consist of all of the following EXCEPT:

A. Corticosteroids

B. Sulfasalazine (5-ASA)

C. Methotrexate

D. Azathioprine

E. Mycophenolate

QUESTION 32

Six months later, you are called to the emergency department to see the same patient who has presented with nausea, vomiting, abdominal pain, and distention. You obtain a water soluble enteroclysis. The cause of the patient's bowel obstruction is:

A. Fistula

B. Abscess

C. Stricture

D. Volvulus

E. Appendicitis

QUESTION 33

Immediate management for the above patient consists of:

A. Immediate laparotomy

B. Nasogastric decompression and IV fluid resuscitation

C. Immediate laparoscopic lysis of adhesions

D. ERCP to evaluate for biliary stenosis

E. This condition does not require intervention

QUESTION 34

Surgical treatment for this patient consists of:

A. Laparotomy with segmental resection

B. Laparotomy with longitudinal enterotomy converted into a transverse closure (stricturoplasty)

C. Laparotomy with side-to-side intestinal bypass

D. Laparoscopic lysis of adhesions

E. Laparoscopic segmental intestinal dilation

BLOCK **TWO**

QUESTIONS

Setting II: Office

Your office is in a primary care generalist group practice located in a physician office suite adjoining a suburban community hospital. Patients are usually seen by appointment. Most of the patients you see are from your own practice and are appearing for regularly scheduled, return visits with some new patients. As in most group practices, you will encounter a patient whose primary care is managed by one of your associates; reference may be made to the patient's medical records. You may do some telephone management and you may have to respond to questions about articles in magazines and on TV that will require interpretation. The laboratory and radiology services are complete.

QUESTION 35

A 74-year-old woman presents to your office with a 12-hr history of right lower leg pain. All of the following physical findings suggest acute arterial insufficiency EXCEPT:

A. Inability of the patient to move her foot

B. Lack of dorsalis pedis or posterior tibial pulse

C. Ulceration over the medial malleolus

D. A cool foot

E. Pallor

QUESTION 36

Six hours after an embolectomy the above patient complains of pain in the right calf. This is not improved with IV morphine. The least sensitive sign or symptom of compartment syndrome is:

A. Increased pain with passive dorsiflexion of the foot

B. Measured pressure of 35 in the deep posterior compartment

C. Decreased sensation in the first toe web space

D. Absent pedal pulses

E. A lower extremity that is firm to palpation

QUESTION 37

A 70-year-old man presents for his annual physical exam. He is in good health with no recent hospitalizations and no prior surgery. He takes no prescription medications and has no allergies. Urinalysis is notable for microscopic hematuria. Cystography is normal. Ultrasound reveals a 3-cm solid left renal mass. CT scan reveals a tumor consistent with renal cell carcinoma. There is evidence of tumor within the renal vein and obvious invasion into the duodenum, pancreas, and aorta. The appropriate next step in the management of this patient is:

A. Percutaneous fine needle aspirate

B. Percutaneous core biopsy

C. Laparoscopic biopsy

D. Endoscopic ultrasound

E. None of the above

QUESTION 38

The most appropriate therapy for the above patient is:

A. Radical nephrectomy with resection of adjacent involved organs

B. Cisplatin-based chemotherapy

C. Nephrectomy only if local symptoms are intolerable

D. High dose IL-2 chemotherapy

E. External beam radiation

QUESTION 39

A 26-year-old man comes to your office complaining of a "new mole" on his right shoulder. He is pale with blonde hair and reports that he has had a significant, chronic, sun exposure. You perform a physical exam and find no palpable lymph nodes. You then perform an excision of the pigmented lesion. Which of the following is NOT true?

A. Melanoma incidence has tripled in the last three decades.

B. Early detection significantly improves the results of treatment.

C. A shave biopsy could have also been performed.

D. Other worrisome characteristics of the lesion would be a change in color, itching, or bleeding.

E. All of the above.

QUESTION 40

The pathology report for the above patient has come back as melanoma with the closest margin at 2 mm. Which of the following is the most helpful for determining prognosis?

A. Clark microstaging

B. Palpable lymph nodes

C. Breslow microstaging

D. Size of the tumor

E. None of the above

QUESTION 41

The next step in treatment for this patient should be:

A. No further therapy

B. Wide excision

C. Wide excision and sentinel lymph node biopsy

D. Wide excision and lymph node dissection

E. Sentinel lymph node biopsy alone

QUESTION 42

A 67-year-old man has had progressive sense of decreased energy. He has a 3-year history of exertional chest discomfort and has had two syncopal episodes over the last 2 years. He presents to your office complaining of shortness of breath, and on your exam, you note lower extremity edema, a harsh systolic murmur, and bibasilar crackles. You are concerned that the patient has aortic stenosis and obtain an echocardiogram, which confirms aortic stenosis and reveals an ejection fraction of 40% and a valve area of 1.2 cm^2/m^2. The factor that confers the worst prognosis if this lesion is not repaired is:

A. Syncope

B. Angina

C. Congestive heart failure

D. Valve area

E. Age

QUESTION 43

The above patient wants to know what his expected survival is if he decides not to proceed with surgery. The best estimate of his survival without surgery given his clinical situation is:

A. 2 years

B. 4 years

C. 5 years

D. 1 year

E. 3 years

QUESTION 44

All of the following are indications for valve replacement EXCEPT:

A. Congestive heart failure

B. Syncope

C. Angina

D. Transaortic gradient of 30 mm Hg

E. Valve area <0.8 cm^2/m^2

QUESTION 45

A 35-year-old female presents to your office with a long history of peptic ulcer disease and is currently on H2 antagonists. She states that she continues to have epigastric pain, had dark stools last week, and now has constant diarrhea. She also complains of fatigue, headache, double vision, and muscle pain that she attributes to marital stress. (She has been unsuccessful with becoming pregnant for over 3 years.) Her initial routine labs are: Na$^+$: 145, K$^+$: 3.5, Cl$^-$: 105, CO$_2$: 24, Glucose: 96, Mg$^+$: 2.0, Ca$^+$: 9.8, HCT: 29. Additional test(s) needed to obtain the diagnosis is/are:

A. Secretin stimulation test, PTH

B. PTH alone

C. Dexamethasone suppression test

D. C-peptide:insulin ratio

E. Serum somatostatin

QUESTION 46

Which of the following should be addressed first as you care for the above patient:

A. Enucleation of the gastrinoma after successful localization by CT scan

B. Total parathyroidectomy with autotransplantation for hyperparathyroidism

C. Excision of the pituitary adenoma

D. Subtotal pancreatectomy for insulinoma

E. Debulking and/or resection of somatostatinoma

QUESTION 47

Your treatment efforts for the patient above are successful. Two years later, on follow-up, the patient brings her 1-year-old son along with her to clinic. She asks if there is anything she needs to know about this condition as it relates to her son. You tell her:

A. There is no genetic predisposition for her disease.

B. He will most likely require a proton pump inhibitor by the time he is 18 years old.

C. Screening is indicated for the family of patients with this disease.

D. Proper diet and exercise will prevent the occurrence of this disease in her children.

QUESTION 48

You are caring for an elderly man with chronic lymphocytic leukemia (CLL) who complains of intermittent severe abdominal pain and fullness with progressive early satiety and weight loss. Labs show a Hct of 25 despite repeat transfusions, and exam reveals massive splenomegaly that his oncologist feels is limiting ongoing medical treatment of his CLL. The most appropriate next step in the management of this patient is:

A. Emergent splenectomy

B. More chemotherapy

C. Elective splenectomy

D. Intravenous gamma globulin

E. Steroids

QUESTION 49

A 68-year-old man presents to your office complaining of a sore on his left lower lip. He thinks that this has been present for at least a month although his wife states that he has been complaining about it for at least 2 months or more. His medical history is notable for hypertension and coronary artery disease. He is 5 years status post partial cystectomy for bladder cancer. He has a 60-pack year smoking history and is a recovering alcoholic. You are appropriately concerned that this may be a squamous cell cancer of the oral cavity. Biopsy confirms this diagnosis. Which one or more of the following are necessary in the preoperative evaluation of this patient?

A. CT scan of the neck

B. Chest x-ray

C. Endoscopy of the nasopharynx, oropharynx, and larynx

D. Esophagoscopy

E. No further workup is necessary prior to surgical resection

QUESTION 50

Which of the following is not a risk factor for squamous cell carcinoma of the head and neck?

A. Tobacco use

B. Alcohol use

C. Poor oral hygiene

D. Ultraviolet light

E. All of the above are risk factors

QUESTION 51

Your above patient has a 1-cm tumor without evidence of adenopathy or distant metastasis. Which one or more of the following is appropriate therapy for this tumor?

A. Surgical excision alone

B. Radiation therapy alone

C. Surgical excision and radiation therapy

D. Chemotherapy

E. Radiation and chemotherapy

QUESTION 52

A 32-year-old mother of three brings her youngest child, a 3-year-old boy, to your office because she noted swelling of his abdomen while she was giving him a bath. She has not noted any other symptoms. You evaluate the child and note a large, easily palpable, left-sided solid mass. You are appropriately concerned about cancer. The cancer most likely to be found in this boy is:

A. Nephroblastoma

B. Neuroblastoma

C. Teratoma

D. Rhabdomyosarcoma

E. Malignant fibrous histiocytoma

QUESTION 53

You perform a CT scan on the above patient that reveals an 8-cm tumor with calcification that appears to be arising from the gland of origin. At surgery you perform a resection that completely removes the tumor, which confirms that the tumor was in fact confined to the gland of origin. The patient's mother eagerly awaits information regarding further therapy and prognosis. You tell her:

A. The patient is cured and can expect a 100% 5-year survival.

B. Chemotherapy is required and the patient has an 80% chance of surviving 5 years.

C. Chemotherapy is required and the patient has a 50% chance of surviving 5 years.

D. Radiotherapy is required and the patient has an 80% chance of surviving 5 years.

E. Radiotherapy is required and the patient has a 50% chance of surviving 5 years.

QUESTION 54

A 55-year-old man presents to your office with a complaint of abdominal pain. This has been getting worse over the past 24 hr. He complains of associated nausea and bilious vomiting. He has not been able to eat solids or drink liquids without vomiting for the last 12 hr. The patient last passed flatus on the car trip to see you. The patient's medical history is notable for hypertension, gout, and colon cancer. He is 7 years status post right hemicolectomy and adjuvant chemotherapy for a Duke's B2 colon cancer. T-36.8, HR-90, RR-16, BP-155/89. WBC-7000, Amylase-65. The abdomen is distended, tympanitic, quiet, and mildly, but diffusely tender, without localized tenderness. You obtain these abdominal films (see Figure 54). The most likely cause of this man's problem is:

A. Recurrent local colon cancer

B. Colorectal metastasis

C. Adhesive band

D. Primary small bowel tumor

E. Ileus

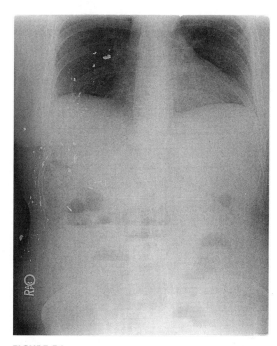

FIGURE 54

QUESTION 55

The most appropriate next step in the management of this patient is:

A. Exploratory laparotomy

B. Exploratory laparoscopy

C. CT scan

D. Hospital admission, IV fluid, and nasogastric tube decompression

E. Hospital admission, IV fluid, nasogastric decompression, and IV broad spectrum antibiotics

QUESTION 56

Which of the following are indications to proceed with immediate operative exploration in this patient?

A. Persistent focal tenderness

B. Fever

C. Elevated white blood cell count

D. Tachycardia

E. All of the above

QUESTION 57

A 45-year-old woman presents to your office complaining of abdominal pain. She has had several episodes in the past 6 months of cramping, postprandial, right-sided pain that lasts several hours. A previous ultrasound documented gallstones. Past medical history is otherwise unremarkable. In the office today: T-37.6, HR-80, RR-13, BP-125/85. WBC-9000, ALT-55, AST-65, total bili-1.1. Abdominal exam is notable for obesity. There is no focal tenderness, and no masses or peritoneal signs. The most likely diagnosis in this patient is:

A. Symptomatic cholelithiasis

B. Acute cholecystitis

C. Choledocholithiasis

D. Ascending cholangitis

E. Biliary dyskinesia

QUESTION 58

The most appropriate test to confirm acute cholecystitis in the above patient is:

A. Abdominal ultrasound

B. Abdominal CT scan

C. Oral cholecystogram

D. HIDA scan

E. Percutaneous transhepatic cholangiography

QUESTION 59

A 40-year-old man comes to your office complaining of left scrotal swelling. He states that it has been this way for 1 week. He initially noticed the swelling shortly after moving furniture for his wife. He reports no nausea, vomiting, change in bowel habits, abdominal pain, or urinary tract symptoms. On examination he has an enlarged left scrotum that is easily reduced, and when the patient is asked to valsalva you feel a protrusion at the internal ring. He most likely has:

A. An incarcerated indirect inguinal hernia

B. A strangulated indirect inguinal hernia

C. A direct inguinal hernia

D. An indirect inguinal hernia

E. A pantaloon hernia

QUESTION 60

The procedure of choice for this patient is:

A. Stoppa procedure

B. Lichtenstein procedure

C. McVay procedure

D. Bassini procedure

QUESTION 61

Complications related to inguinal hernia repair include all of the following EXCEPT:

A. Recurrent hernia

B. Chronic pain

C. Testicular ischemia

D. Long-term urinary tract problems

QUESTION 62

A 79-year-old male comes to your office complaining of dark urine. He is quite healthy with no past surgical history and is presently not taking prescription medications. He recently finished a course of antibiotics for a UTI. He has a 50-pack year history of smoking. Physical exam is benign. Urinalysis shows RBCs present and no WBCs. CT scan shows no stones or renal masses. Cystoscopy and biopsy reveal a transitional cell bladder tumor that does not appear to be advanced. Appropriate treatment is:

A. Chemotherapy

B. Chemotherapy and radiation therapy

C. Transurethral resection with chemotherapy

D. Radical cystectomy

E. Radical cystectomy with radiation and chemotherapy

BLOCK **THREE**

QUESTIONS

Setting III: In-Patient Facilities

You have general admitting privileges to the hospital. You may see patients in the critical care unit or the pediatrics unit or the maternity unit or in recovery. You may also be called to see patients in the psychiatric unit. There is a short-stay unit for patients undergoing same-day operations or being held for observation. There are adjacent nursing home/extended-care facilities and a detoxification unit where you may see patients.

QUESTION 63

A 55-year-old man is admitted to the hospital with a long history of alcohol abuse and hepatitis C. He is a known cirrhotic with ascites controlled by medication; his total bilirubin is 1.8. He has no encephalopathy, good nutritional status, and a serum albumin of 3.2. He is admitted with his second hemodynamically significant variceal bleed in the last 6 months. Esophageal banding is performed, but the patient rebleeds while in the hospital and has a second variceal banding procedure. The most appropriate next step in the treatment of this patient is:

A. Transjugular intrahepatic portocaval shunt

B. Selective operative portocaval shunt

C. Nonselective operative portocaval shunt

D. Endoscopic sclerotherapy

E. None of the above

QUESTION 64

The above patient lives on a farm 90 miles from the nearest health care facility and 150 miles from your institution. You elect to perform a portocaval shunt for esophageal decompression. All of the following are benefits to performing a nonselective shunt EXCEPT:

A. Decreased incidence of encephalopathy

B. Technically less demanding

C. Not dependent on splenic vein anatomy

D. Lower incidence of failure (repeat variceal bleed)

QUESTION 65

This patient's expected operative mortality for a portocaval shunt is:

A. 2%

B. 10%

C. 20%

D. 50%

E. 80%

QUESTION 66

You have just performed a quadruple coronary artery bypass on a 76-year-old, male diabetic with a preoperative cardiac ejection fraction of 25%. You obtained a complete revascularization with grafts to the left anterior descending artery, the first diagonal, the first and second obtuse marginals, and the right coronary artery. The patient is having a difficult time being weaned from cardiopulmonary bypass despite optimizing volume status and appropriate use of inotropic agents. The next appropriate step in managing this situation is:

A. Insertion of an intra-aortic balloon pump

B. Insertion of a left ventricular assist device

C. Place another bypass graft

D. Continue with current efforts and increase inotropic support

E. Insertion of a biventricular assist device

QUESTION 67

Which one of the following is an absolute contraindication to the appropriate management step chosen above?

A. Mitral stenosis

B. Mitral regurgitation

C. Aortic stenosis

D. Aortic insufficiency

E. None of the above

QUESTION 68

On afternoon rounds you note that your 45-year-old patient, who is 6 days status post-total colectomy for ulcerative colitis has some erythema around his wound. He notes that it is a bit more tender today, but he is otherwise well and beginning to tolerate his diet. You decide simply to watch the wound carefully and check back first thing in the morning. When you do, the erythema is unchanged and a very small amount of purulent drainage is now emanating from the center of the erythematous portion of the wound. The most appropriate therapy at this time is:

A. Start cefazolin

B. Start cephalexin

C. Open and pack the wound

D. Open and pack the wound and start cefazolin

E. Open and pack the wound and start cephalexin

QUESTION 69

You are asked to consult on a 72-year-old female who is 6 days status post placement of dynamic hip screw of the right hip. She has had no stool or flatus since surgery. On exam, you note generalized lethargy and abdominal distention. She seems to have no pain on abdominal palpation and percussion (which is tympanitic). Her past medical history is significant for coronary artery disease and a left-sided stroke 10 days ago. Laboratory data obtained shows: Na^+: 137, K^+: 2.9, Cl^-: 130, CO_2: 23, Mg^{2+}: 0.7. Plain abdominal films are obtained. Your diagnosis is:

A. Colonic volvulus

B. Small bowel obstruction

C. Acute pseudo-obstruction (Ogilvie's syndrome)

D. Acute appendicitis

E. Ileus

QUESTION 70

You recommend correction of this patient's electrolytes and:

A. Immediate laparoscopy

B. Immediate laparotomy

C. Administration of neostigmine if there are no contraindications

D. Immediate water soluble enema

E. Immediate observation

QUESTION 71

To prevent this condition from recurring you suggest:

A. Cecostomy

B. Cecopexy

C. Right hemicolectomy

D. Monitor electrolyte abnormalities and metabolic derangements and avoid narcotics

E. Total abdominal colectomy

BLOCK **FOUR**

QUESTIONS

Setting IV: Emergency Department

Generally patients encountered here are seeking urgent care and most are not known to you. Available to you are a full range of social services, including rape crisis intervention, family support, child protective services, domestic violence support, psychiatric services, and security assistance backed up by local police. Complete laboratory and radiology services are available.

QUESTION 72

A 68-year-old man presents to the emergency room with a 2-hr history of diffuse abdominal pain that was associated with an episode of near syncope. HR-110, BP-90/60, RR-22, T-36.5. Abdominal exam is remarkable for a pulsatile abdominal mass. The most appropriate next step in the management of this patient is:

A. Obtain a helical CT scan

B. Obtain a lower extremity duplex

C. Alert the operating room

D. Obtain an aortogram

E. Obtain an abdominal ultrasound

QUESTION 73

A 78-year-old man presents to the emergency room having had several episodes of bright red blood per rectum over the past 2 hr. He is hypotensive and tachycardic. However, this resolves after he receives 1500 cc of crystalloid infusion. A nasogastric aspirate reveals bile and no blood. The most likely etiology of this man's bleeding is:

A. Colon cancer

B. Angiodysplasia

C. Peptic ulcer

D. Diverticulitis

E. Diverticulosis

QUESTION 74

You want to use the test that gives you the best chance to document the above patient's bleeding, or the most sensitive one. You therefore order:

A. Tagged red blood cell scan

B. Visceral angiography

C. Colonoscopy

D. Esophagogastroduodenoscopy

E. Serial hematocrits

QUESTION 75

A 55-year-old diabetic, who is status post renal transplantation and coronary artery bypass surgery, presents to the ER with rectal pain. The patient's medical history is notable for hypertension, hyperlipidemia, and congestive heart failure. The pain has been present and getting worse for 36 hr. Physical exam reveals: T-37.0, HR-85, BP-155/90, RR-14. The abdomen is soft, nontender, and nondistended. Rectal exam is well-tolerated and notable for a laterally located, fluctuant mass. The most appropriate therapy for this problem is:

A. Oral antibiotics and follow-up in 24 hr

B. Admission for IV antibiotics

C. Stab incision and drainage in the ER with admission and IV antibiotics

D. Incision and drainage in the operating room and IV antibiotics

E. None of the above

QUESTION 76

An 18-year-old woman is brought to the emergency room for intermittent stupor, marked confusion, and a flapping tremor. Vitals-stable. PT-24. INR-3.5. Total bili-4.5. Direct bili-1.0. Glucose-30. Intravenous glucose does not improve her mental status. You suspect that she has acute fulminant hepatic failure. The most common etiology of AFHF in the United States is:

A. Hepatitis B

B. Hepatitis A

C. Toxin

D. Hepatitis C

E. Idiopathic

QUESTION 77

Which one or more of the following is/are a potential secondary effect of AFHF?

A. Profound hypoglycemia

B. Cardiovascular collapse

C. Increased intracranial pressure

D. Hyperkalemia

E. All of the above

QUESTION 78

A 68-year-old man presents to the emergency room complaining of right upper quadrant abdominal pain of 3 days duration and shaking chills every 8 hr for 24 hr. Past medical history is significant for hypertension, hyperlipidemia, and right calf claudication. He has been hospitalized twice for diverticulitis, most recently 1 month ago. He has a remote history of open cholecystectomy. The patient is hemodynamically stable although slightly somnolent. He awakens to voice and answers questions appropriately. Lungs are clear and the abdomen is notable for right upper quadrant tenderness. Abdominal CT scan reveals a single well-demarcated lesion in the right lobe of the liver, without any other intra-abdominal pathology. This most likely represents:

A. Colorectal metastasis

B. Pyogenic abscess

C. Amebic abscess

D. Hepatocellular carcinoma

E. Hemangioma

QUESTION 79

Appropriate therapy for the patient above is:

A. Exploratory laparotomy and resection of the mass

B. Broad spectrum IV antibiotics

C. Broad spectrum IV antibiotics and percutaneous drainage

D. Broad spectrum IV antibiotics and surgical drainage

E. None of the above

QUESTION 80

A 34-year-old man, who immigrated from Honduras 6 months ago, presents to the ER with a 1-month history of vague abdominal pain, low-grade fever, occasional chills, and decreased appetite. In the ER the patient is hemodynamically stable. T-38. ALT/AST-1.2X normal. Total bili-1.1. Indirect hemoagglutination is positive to 1:512 dilution and abdominal ultrasound reveals a 7-cm lesion in the right lobe of the liver. (See Figure 80.) The best initial management for this problem is:

A. IV ampicillin/gentamycin/metronidazole

B. PO metronidazole

C. PO metronidazole + percutaneous drainage

D. PO metronidazole + operative drainage

E. IV ampicillin/gentamycin/metronidazole + operative drainage

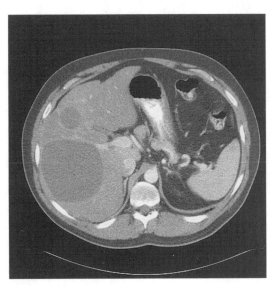

FIGURE 80

QUESTION 81

A 23-year-old male was an ejected passenger in a motor vehicle crash. He is transported by ground ambulance and arrives 30 min after the crash. During transport he received 3 liters of NS. On arrival he complains of abdominal pain and is somewhat somnolent. Vitals on arrival: HR-120, BP-80/60, RR-22, T-36. His exam is remarkable for facial abrasions, a distended and tender abdomen, marked deformity of his right femur, and generalized pallor. After performing the ABCs, the most appropriate next step is:

A. Transfuse O-negative blood

B. CT scan

C. DPL

D. Chest x-ray

E. Infuse 2 liters of saline rapidly

QUESTION 82

An 18-year-old boy suffered a direct blow to his right arm during a football game. He presents to the emergency room complaining of right arm pain. The pain is exacerbated by abduction and adduction of the arm. Radiograph of the upper arm demonstrates a displaced distal humerus fracture. The most likely associated injury is:

A. Radial nerve injury

B. Ulnar nerve injury

C. Scaphoid fracture

D. Lunate fracture

E. Brachial artery injury

QUESTION 83

A 26-year-old male restrained driver involved in a motor vehicle crash at highway speed with two associated fatalities arrives in your emergency room intubated and sedated. Vitals: HR-90, BP-120/80, T-36.2, RR-18 (mechanical ventilation). He has an obvious right femur fracture and sternal ecchymosis. You obtain the following radiograph (see Figure 83). This study makes you concerned about the possibility of:

A. Pneumothorax

B. Tracheobronchial injury

C. Aortic disruption

D. Splenic laceration

E. Diaphragmatic injury

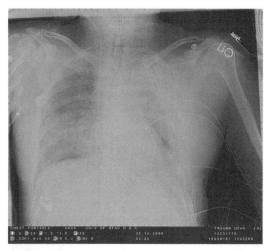

FIGURE 83

QUESTION 84

The gold standard for diagnosing this injury (see Figure 84) is:

A. Transesophageal echocardiogram

B. Helical CT scan of the chest

C. Aortic angiography

D. Chest x-ray

E. None of the above

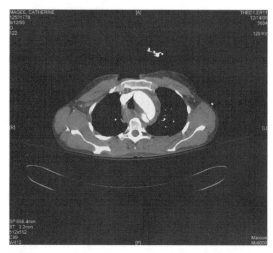

FIGURE 84

QUESTION 85

A 50-year-old male presents to the emergency room with a history of 24 hr of fever and vomiting. He has localized tenderness in the right lower quadrant, about two-thirds of the way between his iliac crest and his umbilicus. You suspect appendicitis and perform laparoscopic appendectomy without incident. The pathology report indicates the existence of a 5-cm mass at the base of the appendix. The patient returns to your clinic for follow-up and reports a 6-month history of anorexia, weight loss, and fatigue. Although he does not smoke, he states that he has had increasing occurrences of wheezing and feeling flush. His wife thinks he has a new allergy to spicy food because of his frequent liquid stool and flushed appearance after meals. This scenario is most consistent with:

A. Celiac disease

B. Metastatic colon adenocarcinoma

C. Carcinoid

D. Insulinoma

E. Gastrinoma

QUESTION 86

When discussing your thoughts with this patient you indicate that you are concerned because of his symptoms and because:

A. The tumor size is greater than 2 cm.

B. The tumor size is greater than 4 cm.

C. Celiac disease is immunosuppressive.

D. Appendiceal tumors of this type are more aggressive than midgut tumors of similar histology.

QUESTION 87

You confirm your diagnosis of the above patient with:

A. Colonoscopy

B. Serum serotonin

C. Urine metanephrines

D. Barium enema

E. Chest x-ray

QUESTION 88

After confirming the diagnosis, a CT scan of the abdomen is obtained (see Figure 88) and demonstrates multiple lesions in both lobes of the liver. Your treatment plan could consist of all the following except:

A. Surgical resection

B. Octreotide

C. Alpha-interferon

D. Radiation to the liver

E. 5-FU

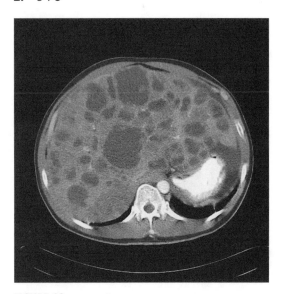

FIGURE 88

QUESTION 89

A 16-year-old male comes to the emergency department complaining of 1 hr of severe left testicular pain and swelling. He is sexually active and is worried about an infection. On examination you note an exquisitely tender, swollen left testicle that is somewhat elevated. The most appropriate next step in the management of this problem is:

A. Send a urinalysis with culture.

B. Send a urethral swab for gonococcus and chlamydia.

C. Order a duplex ultrasound to evaluate testicular blood flow.

D. All of the above.

QUESTION 90

The duplex confirms that there is no blood flow to the left testicle of the above patient. The next step is:

A. Try to untwist the testicle in the emergency department

B. Surgical exploration and orchiopexy

C. Surgical exploration and orchiopexy of both testis

D. None of the above

QUESTION 91

You are called in to evaluate a trauma victim. While you are waiting for the patient to arrive you find out that the patient is a 36-year-old woman who was the restrained front seat passenger in a T-bone crash at highway speeds to the passenger side. There were two deaths at the scene. The patient arrives intubated and hypotensive with a SBP of 70 and a HR of 60. Your first priority is to:

A. Check an end-tidal CO_2 to check proper endotracheal tube placement.

B. Ask the paramedics more details about the accident.

C. Place a central line, so you can give blood.

D. Listen for breath sounds.

QUESTION 92

You determine that the ET tube is in proper position, get IV access, and palpate multiple right sided rib fractures with associated crepitance. Her SBP is now 60 and HR is 50. Your next step is:

A. CT scan of head, chest, and abdomen

B. Chest x-ray to rule out pneumothorax

C. Emergent right chest tube

D. Right thoracotomy and aortic clamping

QUESTION 93

A 49-year-old male presents to the emergency department complaining of severe abdominal pain. He tells you that he has had intermittent epigastric pain for several months, but today the pain suddenly worsened. He is an alcoholic who drinks over a pint of alcohol a day and reports that he takes no medications except ibuprofen. Examination reveals diffuse abdominal pain with guarding. WBC is 14,000 and you obtain this x-ray (see Figure 93). You take him to the operating room for emergent laparotomy and find a perforated gastric ulcer. Your next step is to:

A. Oversew the ulcer

B. Excisional biopsy of the ulcer and closure of the ulcer

C. Close the patient and start a proton pump inhibitor

D. Antrectomy

E. None of the above

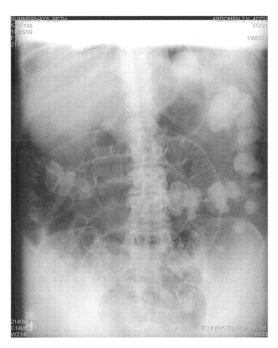

FIGURE 93

QUESTION 94

A 40-year-old male comes to the emergency department complaining of right-sided abdominal pain that radiates to his right testicle. When you see him he appears very uncomfortable, moving all around on the bed. He reports that he has been vomiting and has noted blood in his urine. Physical exam revels no hernias, abdomen is soft without guarding, and urinalysis shows the presence of RBCs, but no WBCs. (See Figure 94.) This patient most likely has:

A. An acute abdomen

B. Urinary tract infection

C. Ureteral stones

D. Prostatitis

E. None of the above

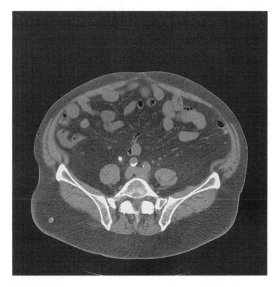

FIGURE 94

QUESTION 95

To further work up this problem, all of the following are appropriate except:

A. Abdominal CT scan with contrast

B. Abdominal x-ray

C. Intravenous pyelogram

D. Retrograde pyelogram

QUESTION 96

The most common type of kidney stone is

A. Uric acid

B. Struvite

C. Calcium oxalate

D. Cystine

QUESTION 97A

A 65-year-old male presents to the emergency department with a 36-hr history of nausea and vomiting. He is lethargic and does not remember when he had his last bowel movement. He has a medical history of hypertension and coronary artery disease and no surgical history. Vital signs are as follows: BP-105/68, Resp-32, Pulse-72, O_2 sat 98%. His abdomen is markedly distended and tender. You are unable to palpate any hernia. Abdominal films are consistent with small bowel obstruction. The most common cause of small bowel obstruction in this patient is:

A. Hernias

B. Adhesions

C. Malignancy

D. Foreign body

E. Inflammatory bowel disease

QUESTION 97B

After initial resuscitation with fluid and electrolytes, as well as placement of a nasogastric tube, the most appropriate next step in the management of this patient is:

A. Admission for 24-hr period of attempted spontaneous resolution

B. Upper GI contrast study to evaluate for complete obstruction

C. Exploratory laparotomy

D. Barium enema to evaluate for colon cancer

E. Bedside abdominal ultrasonography

QUESTION 98

A small bowel tumor is found to be the cause of the above patient's small bowel obstruction. Appropriate treatment was instituted. The patient improves and is discharged. Six months later he presents with similar symptoms. His plain abdominal films show multiple air fluid levels. After initial resuscitation with appropriate fluid and electrolytes as well as placement of nasogastric tube, the most appropriate next step in the management of this patient is:

A. Enteroclysis

B. Abdominal CT scan with contrast

C. Abdominal ultrasound

D. Colonoscopy

E. No treatment. Obtain a hospice referral. His obstruction is due to recurrent cancer.

QUESTION 99

The initial appropriate management is adminis-tered. On radiographic exam, there is no evidence of obstructing or recurrent mass. However, the patient continues to have high NG output and obstipation. After resuscitation, he remains hemodynamically stable with a normal lactate and good mentation. It would be appropriate for this patient to undergo:

A. An initial period of observation for sponta-neous resolution

B. Exploratory laparoscopy

C. Exploratory laparotomy

D. Enteroclysis for therapeutic resolution

E. Ampicillin, gentamycin, and metronidazole administration

QUESTION 100A

The patient improves after appropriate man-agement. He is concerned about a recurrence of his condition. In your counseling, you tell him:

A. He has a 5–10% recurrence rate

B. He has a 10–15% recurrence rate

C. He has a 25–40% recurrence rate

D. He has a 60–75% recurrence rate

E. He has greater than 90% chance of recur-rence

QUESTION 100B

With regard to adhesions, the strongest predic-tor for future obstruction is:

A. Number of previous recurrences

B. Type of adhesions (single or matted)

C. Type of initial surgery

D. Whether lysis of adhesions is performed on the entire bowel

E. The use of hand sewn anastomosis.

BLOCK **ONE**

ANSWERS

ANSWER 1

A. A small but significant subset of patients with metastatic colorectal cancer will be cured with resection of liver metastases. Predictors of a positive response to surgical resection include: duration of disease free interval >1 year, node negative primary, single lesion and lesion size <2 cm. Since this patient is young, healthy, and has a single small lesion in the left lateral segment which presented 30 months after his initial diagnosis, he is a good candidate for liver resection. Repeat administration of 5-FU/leucovorin is not indicated. If the patient were not a candidate for liver resection because of medical comorbidity then no further therapy would be a reasonable course. Anatomic resection is the preferred operation. It can be accomplished, in this case, with a left lateral segmentectomy, which will leave adequate residual hepatic tissue. (See Figure 1.)

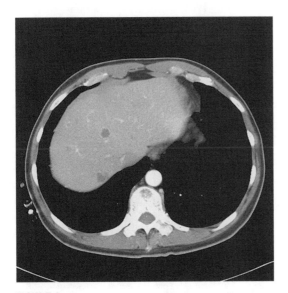

FIGURE 1

ANSWER 2

C. The most common benign tumor of the liver is hemangioma. These typically present in young women. The differential for benign liver tumors includes FNH and adenoma, which also typically occur in young women. Oral contraceptives are a risk factor for hepatic adenoma.

ANSWER 3

E. Hepatic adenomas carry a 10% risk of malignant degeneration as well as the risk of spontaneous rupture and bleeding which can be life threatening. For these reasons most hepatic adenomas ultimately require resection. A minority of these tumors will regress with the cessation of oral estrogens; therefore, small minimally symptomatic lesions can be followed in the absence of estrogens rather than proceeding directly with surgery.

ANSWER 4

E. Urinalysis is an important first step in the workup of hematuria. One must be concerned about a urinary tract tumor and the first step is to document gross or microscopic hematuria.

ANSWER 5

A. When confronted with this lesion that is consistent with a transitional cell cancer of the bladder, one should completely resect it through the cystoscope (transurethral resection of bladder tumor, TURBT). This procedure allows staging of the lesion and will determine whether further therapy is warranted. Transitional tumors comprise approximately 90% of all bladder tumors. Approximately 70% of transitional tumors are superficial while the other 30% are invasive or metastatic. Patients in whom the tumor does not invade past the lamina propria do not typically receive adjuvant therapy. However, patients with TA and T1 tumors (not invading past the lamina propria) who may be candidates for adjuvant intravesicular chemotherapy include those with high-grade lesions, aneuploid tumors, tumors >5 cm, and those with persistently positive cytology. These patients require close follow-up, as up to 50% of patients will develop recurrent disease, although it recurs at the same stage in the majority of cases.

ANSWER 6

C. The most worrisome pigmented lesion is melanoma, but many other pigmented lesions must also be evaluated. Lesions should be looked at urgently if there is a history of increase in the size of the lesion, change in coloration (either lighter or darker), and any suggestion of bleeding or ulceration. An excisional biopsy is the correct procedure and a border of noninvolved skin should be included. All of the following require excisional biopsy: congenital giant nevus, pigmented basal cell carcinoma, Kaposi's sarcoma, melanoma, spitz nevus, and seborrheic keratoses.

ANSWER 7

A. This lesion is a lung carcinoma until proven otherwise. The next diagnostic step is CT scan of the chest. This allows you to obtain an accurate size of the mass, look for synchronous lesions, and evaluate the lymph nodes for initial staging of the lesion. Chest ultrasound in not useful. Mediastinoscopy is used to obtain lymph node biopsies if there are suspicious, large (>1 cm) nodes seen on CT. FNA can obtain cells to arrive at a cytologic diagnosis. While malignant cells confirms malignancy, the absence of malignant cells does not necessarily rule out malignancy and further diagnostic steps must be taken including thoracoscopy or thoracotomy.

ANSWER 8

A. One goal of the pre-operative work-up for lung resection candidates is to determine whether they will have adequate residual lung parenchyma after surgery so that they will not be ventilator dependent. A number of tests can help with this determination. The most important is the forced expiratory volume in one second (FEV1). The absolute minimum FEV1 is 0.8 L. Some authors suggest a cutoff of 1.0 L. Marginal candidates can undergo ventilation perfusion scanning. In some cases, the lung that is to be removed is not contributing to ventilation because the tumor already occludes the bronchus. V/Q scan will demonstrate this situation making you more comfortable that the patient will tolerate the resection. Arterial hypoxemia and hypercarbia are relative contraindications, but in and of themselves do not preclude resection. Vital capacity does not play a role in the decision regarding the patients' competency for lung resection.

ANSWER 9

B.

ANSWER 10

A.

ANSWER 11

B. This patient presents with symptoms of glucagonoma. Most patients with this disease are diabetic and have a history of recent weight loss. The skin condition described in the scenario is referred to as necrolytic migratory dermatitis and is closely associated with this disease condition. Serum glucagon levels greater than 150 pg/ml confirm the diagnosis. The tumor is localized with CT scan and its second most common location is the duodenum. Resection requires enucleation with a rim of normal tissue due to the fact that nearly two-thirds of these tumors are malignant. Only one-third of patients are cured with resection, and chemotherapy or octreotide may be indicated due to the slow growing nature of this tumor. The most common metastatic sites are the liver and nodal basins.

ANSWER 12

B.

ANSWER 13

B. Both of the above patients have immune thrombocytopenic purpura (ITP). This is an immune condition with antiplatelet antibodies. It is most common in women in their 30s and in children under the age of 6 years (typically seen after a viral illness in children). The spleen plays a dual role in this disease. It is the source of the IgG specific for platelets and

the site of the phagocytosis of the coated platelets. The signs and symptoms include: bleeding following minor trauma, easy bruising, mucosal bleeding, and petechiae. The spleen is usually not enlarged. In adults the initial treatment is prednisone, 1 mg/kg/day. Most patients respond to achieve a platelet count greater than 100,000, but only 25% of patients sustain this after the steroid taper. In patients not responsive to steroids, IV immune globulin will temporarily raise the platelet count after 5–7 days. If the patient fails medical therapy, a splenectomy is indicated. Splenectomy is successful therapy in 85% of patients. Favorable responses occur in patients, who initially respond to steroid therapy, are under 60 years old, have a disease of short duration, and exhibit a prompt thrombocytosis after splenectomy. Emergency splenectomy is rarely indicated except for those with central nervous system bleeding. Failure after splenectomy may be due to a missed accessory spleen, which can be documented with a technetium 99 colloid scan or by infusion of indium 111-labeled platelets. If no accessory spleen is documented to account for the failure, one may consider: pulsed high-dose steroids, IgG, cyclosporine, plasmapheresis, chemotherapeutic agents (vincristine, vinblastine, azathioprine, or cyclophosphamide), danazol, or immunoadsorption with staph-protein-A pheresis. In childhood, ITP is typically self-limited (6–12 months) and strict bed rest with avoidance of contact sports is recommended. Splenectomy is indicated in patients who have not had spontaneous remission after 1 year.

ANSWER 14

C.

ANSWER 15

C. This patient has Budd–Chiari syndrome. Budd–Chiari syndrome is defined as occlusion of the hepatic veins and/or suprahepatic inferior vena cava, producing post-sinusoidal portal hypertension that develops secondary to obstruction of hepatic venous drainage. It is characterized by the onset of ascites, abdominal pain, and tender hepatomegaly. If untreated, most patients die of progressive liver failure or succumb to a complication of portal hypertension. There is a preponderance of women affected by this syndrome, who are most often diagnosed in their 30s. Liver function is relatively unperturbed, transaminase and bilirubin levels are usually normal, the alkaline phosphatase level is normal to mildly elevated, and the prothrombin time is normal to slightly prolonged. Elevated protein concentration in the ascitic fluid is suggestive of Budd–Chiari syndrome. Hypoalbuminemia is a relatively consistent finding. The gold standard for diagnosis is hepatic venography. The surgical options for treating patients with hepatic vein thrombosis can be separated into four general categories: peritoneovenous shunts, excision of the venous obstruction, portasystemic decompression, and orthotopic liver transplantation.

ANSWER 16

B.

ANSWER 17

B.

ANSWER 18

C. This is the classic description of a patient with hypertrophic pyloric stenosis. This syndrome is four times more common in male infants than female infants. It is more common in the first-born son and more commonly occurs in the offspring of women who had the disease as children. This typically presents at about 1 month of age with increasing vomiting that progresses to projectile vomiting. The vomitus is nonbilious because the obstruction is proximal to the ampulla of Vater. It is common to have severe electrolyte imbalances secondary to dehydration and surgery must be delayed until these imbalances have been corrected. Prolonged vomiting leads to a hypokalemic, hypochloremic contraction alkalosis as the kidneys try to retain sodium and water at the expense of hydrogen and potassium. The treatment of choice is the Fredet–Ramstedt pyloromyotomy. This procedure is well tolerated with most patients resuming oral intake within 12 hr of surgery.

ANSWER 19

A.

ANSWER 20

C.

ANSWER 21

E. This patient gives a classic history for chronic mesenteric ischemia. "Food fear" is present because of intestinal angina. Oral intake increases blood flow to the intestine. In the setting of a fixed visceral arterial stenosis, the appropriate increase in blood flow cannot be achieved resulting in abdominal pain after meals. This often leads to an avoidance of food and weight loss. The diagnosis is made with visceral angiography. Treatment is individualized to the patient and depends upon the severity of the syndrome, the patient's comorbidities, and the perceived risk/benefit ratio of angioplasty or surgery.

In contrast to this patient, mesenteric ischemia can present acutely. Acute mesenteric ischemia can be caused by arterial thrombosis or embolus, venous occlusion (typically in patients with a hypercoagulable state) or "low flow" nonocclusive mesenteric ischemia. Patients typically have "pain out of proportion" to their physical exam, leukocytosis, and lactic acidosis. This acute condition is associated with exceptionally high mortality, and successful management is contingent upon rapid diagnosis and surgical management. Mesenteric venous occlusion is documented at surgery by edematous bowel and venous clot. Treatment consists of bowel resection and anticoagulation. Venous reconstruction is rarely indicated or successful. Nonocclusive mesenteric ischemia typically occurs in the setting of other acute disease (heart disease, sepsis, etc.) and mesenteric arterial stenosis. Vasoactive medications are often used for hemodynamic support. Arteriography demonstrates the absence of major visceral arterial occlusion. The diagnosis is made at laparotomy. Treatment consists of resection of dead bowel, optimization of volume status, and sometimes intra-arterial vasodilatory therapy (papaverine).

ANSWER 22

E. This patient has an umbilical hernia, which should be repaired surgically on an elective basis. Intestinal obstruction associated with hernias can lead to death and is preventable by surgical repair. Incarcerated and strangulated hernias should be repaired immediately, whereas reducible hernias should be repaired electively. All hernias should be repaired with two exceptions: children under 4 years of age with umbilical hernias may be observed and adults with severe medical problems, such as cirrhotics with ascites, that preclude any anesthesia may be observed.

ANSWER 23

B.

ANSWER 24

C. Benign prostatic hyperplasia (BPH) is a common problem in older men. It is the most common cause of bladder outlet obstruction in men over 50 years of age. Bladder outlet obstruction can lead to urinary tract infections and bladder stones secondary to stasis and eventually renal failure secondary to high-pressure urinary retention. Several tests should be performed to evaluate this problem, including a urinalysis with culture to rule out infection; a serum BUN and creatinine to evaluate renal insufficiency; a postvoid residual to rule out chronic urinary retention; ultrasound is used to evaluate the urinary tract including the prostate size, presence of bladder stones, and hydronephrosis; and a digital rectal exam should always be done to evaluate the size of the prostate and to evaluate for nodules. Medical treatment for BPH includes the use of alpha-antagonists for smooth muscle relaxation of the prostate and bladder neck and 5-alpha-reductase inhibitors to block the conversion of testosterone to dihydrotestosterone without lowering serum levels of circulating testosterone. An important side effect of alpha-antagonists to remember is postural hypotension, which can be very problematic in elderly patients. If medical therapy does not relieve the obstruction, surgical therapy is necessary. The procedure of choice is transurethral resection of the prostate (TURP).

ANSWER 25

C. Cryptorchidism is the failure of normal testicular descent during embryologic development. The incidence is 1–2% in full-term infants and up to 30% in premature babies. Operation is indicated after 1 year. Prior to age one, the testis may continue to descend into the scrotum. The cause is unknown. Undescended testes fail in spermatogenic function, but may continue to secrete androgens. Spermatogenic failure is progressive; therefore, surgical exploration and scrotal placement of the testis should be performed before 2-years of age. If placement of the testicle into the scrotum is not possible, then orchiectomy is indicated because of the high risk of testicular cancer when the testis is left in an intra-abdominal position. The incidence of testicular cancer in an abdominal testis is 30 times higher than the normal population. After 2-years of age orchiectomy is the treatment of choice because of the cancer risk and poor spermatogenesis.

ANSWER 26

D. Testicular tumors are the most common genitourinary malignancy for men 20–35 years old. Almost all neoplasms of the testicle are malignant. Tumors are divided into germ cell or nongerm cell tumors. Germ cell tumors account for 90–95% of all tumors. Nongerm cell tumors arise from Leydig and Sertoli cells and produce excess androgenizing hormones. Germ cell tumors arise from totipotent cells of the seminiferous tubules. Germ cell tumors are categorized by the degree of cellular differentiation to seminoma, embryonal carcinoma, and choriocarcinoma. Seminomas are the most common malignant germ cell tumor. Embryonal carcinoma is usually seen in childhood. Tumors usually present as firm painless testicular masses. About 10% of patients with testicular tumors have a history of cryptorchidism. Nongerm cell tumors can cause precocious puberty and virilism in young males and impotence and gynecomastia in adults secondary to the hormone production. Immediate evaluation should include serum for tumor markers alpha-fetoprotein and beta-human chorionic gonadotropin. Tissue biopsy for definitive diagnosis should also be performed immediately. Surgical treatment is usually orchiectomy with or without retroperitoneal lymph node dissection.

ANSWER 27

D. Renal cancer affects males twice as often as females. Two percent of cancer deaths are attributable to renal cancer. Smoking may be a risk factor for renal cell cancer. There are several types of renal cancer including granular cell, tubular adenocarcinoma, Wilms's tumor, and sarcoma. Patients may present with hematuria and flank pain if there is tumor hemorrhage. Diagnosis is made by CT scan and biopsy is not necessary. Treatment in most cases is a radical nephrectomy.

ANSWER 28
C.

ANSWER 29
A.

ANSWER 30
E.

ANSWER 31
E.

ANSWER 32
C.

ANSWER 33
B.

ANSWER 34

B. Although this patient most likely has Crohn's disease, the diagnosis of most concern and the one that must not be overlooked is colon cancer. It is your job, as the physician, to ensure that this patient does not have cancer. Crohn's disease is a chronic inflammatory disorder of the alimentary tract. Its etiology is currently unknown. Crohn's disease can be rapidly progressive or indolent in its course. There are intermittent exacerbations marked by apthous mucosal ulcers, granulomas, and transmural chronic inflammation with fissures and fistulas. Crohn's disease occurs most commonly between the ages of 15 and 35 years. Patients usually present with abdominal pain, weight loss, and diarrhea. Symptoms usually last from 2–3 years before the diagnosis is confirmed. Extra-abdominal abdominal manifestations can be extensive, but the most common are pyoderma gangrenosum, conjunctivitis, and arthritis. Ankylosing spondylitis is also associated with the disease. Currently there are no genetic or laboratory markers specific for the disease. Comparisons between Crohn's disease and ulcerative colitis are shown below. (See Table 34.)

Medical therapy focuses on suppressing the immune system by use of corticosteroids, sulfasalazine, metronidazole, azathioprine, 6-mercaptopurine, methotrexate, and cyclosporine. Strictures of the small bowel in diseased segments are a common complication from aggressive Crohn's disease. Resections of these segments would eventually lead to short bowel syndrome. Stricturoplasty, a technique in which a longitudinal enterotomy is closed vertically at the site of diseased segments, has been very effective at relieving obstructive symptoms without adverse sequelae.

Table 34

Comparisons Between Crohn's Disease and Ulcerative Colitis

Crohn's Disease	Ulcerative Colitis
Gross appearance	
Transmural involvement	Mucosal involvement
Segmental disease	Continuous disease beginning in rectum
Thickened bowel wall	Normal thickness of bowel wall
Creeping fat	No creeping fat
Pseudopolyps rare	Pseudopolyps common
Small bowel involvement	Rare small bowel involvement
Perianal disease common	Perianal disease uncommon
Histologic appearance	
Crypt abscesses uncommon	Crypt abscesses common
Granulomas present	Granulomas absent
Cobblestoning, fistulas	No cobblestoning, fistulas rare
Pseudopolyps absent	Pseudopolyps present
Deep, narrow ulcers	Shallow, wide ulcers

BLOCK **TWO**

ANSWERS

ANSWER 35

 C.

ANSWER 36

D. Acute arterial insufficiency mandates rapid intervention to avoid permanent sequelae. The diagnosis is made by physical exam and it is characterized by the "five Ps:" pain, pallor, paresthesias, pulselessness, and paralysis. Ulceration over the medial malleolus is most characteristic of chronic venous insufficiency/venous stasis.

Patients are at high risk for developing compartment syndrome when reperfusion follows an extended period of ischemia. Early signs of compartment syndrome include pain out of proportion to exam, decreased sensation in the first web space, and increased pain with passive dorsiflexion of the foot. The diagnosis can be confirmed by measuring compartment pressures with any value above 20 mmHg being abnormal. Patients with compartment syndrome typically do not lose the arterial pulse as compartment pressures would have to be exceedingly high (above systolic arterial pressure) to compromise arterial perfusion. Prompt four compartment fasciotomies is the appropriate treatment.

ANSWER 37

E.

ANSWER 38

C. Renal cell carcinoma can be reliably diagnosed with CT scan and attempts at tissue diagnosis via biopsy are contraindicated. The next step, if the cancer is resectable, is to proceed with the resection. This patient has stage IVa disease with tumor spread to adjacent organs (other than the ipsilateral adrenal). Three-year survival for these patients is less than 10%. Nephrectomy in this situation should be done only for palliation of local symptoms. Renal cell carcinoma is not responsive to cytotoxic chemotherapy. The current experimental focus is on immunotherapy, which should be offered in the setting of a clinical trial. External beam radiation does not play a role in the management of RCC.

ANSWER 39

 C.

ANSWER 40

 C.

ANSWER 41

C. Melanoma incidence has tripled in the last three decades, and it currently affects 5–25 per 100,000 people. Early detection significantly improves the results of treatment. Clinically suspicious lesions include those that change in size or color, itch, or bleed. Five to 10% of melanomas are not pigmented. A full thickness excisional biopsy is the preferred treatment. Shave biopsies should not be performed because they prevent adequate assessment of depth. Breslow microstaging involves measurement of the primary melanoma thickness with an ocular micrometer. Clark microstaging method involves histologic determination of the level of invasion into the dermal layers or subcutaneous fat. Tumor thickness (Breslow staging) is a more accurate index of metastatic potential than Clark's level of invasion. Breslow staging is divided as follows: <0.76 mm, 0.76–1.49 mm, 1.50–3.99 mm, and >3.99 mm. This is important in staging for prognosis, the risk of regional and distant metastases, and incidence of local recurrence after 5-year follow-up.

ANSWER 42

C.

ANSWER 43

A.

ANSWER 44

D. Survival with aortic stenosis without surgery has been well defined. The worst prognostic sign is left heart failure. Once this has become clinically evident the patient's average survival is 2 years. Survival after the onset of angina is 5 years and after syncope is 3 years. This accounts for the recommendation to time surgery before or just after there is evidence of change in left ventricular function or dimensions. The 1-year mortality rate after the onset of any symptoms is 25%; the 2-year mortality is 50%. Death is often sudden, which is why surgery is generally recommended after the development of any symptoms. Other indications are a transvalvular gradient of greater than 50 mm Hg and a valve area of <0.8 cm^2/m^2.

ANSWER 45

A.

ANSWER 46

B.

ANSWER 47

C. This patient has MEN I syndrome. The syndrome usually is associated with pituitary adenoma (most commonly prolactinoma), hyperparathyroidism, and pancreatic tumors (most commonly gastrinoma). Prolactinomas can lead to infertility due to the secretion of prolactin interrupting the menstrual cycle. Gastrinomas secrete an abnormal amount of the peptide gastrin that stimulates gastric parietal cells to increase acid secretion leading to ulcer disease. Most gastrinomas are located to the right of the superior mesenteric vessels within the head of the pancreas or the duodenum. Hyperparathyroidism leads to excess serum calcium levels causing neuromuscular, urinary, and gastrointestinal sequelae. Treatment of the hyperparathyroidism should occur first, since this condition exacerbates ulcer disease and can lead to complications during other procedures. Prolactinomas can be treated with bromocriptine and be excised through a transphenoidal approach. Gastrinomas require enucleation from the pancreas when possible, but multiple pancreatic tumors may occur and more extensive resection may be necessary. MEN I syndrome warrants screening in affected families.

ANSWER 48

C. In CLL and CML, splenomegaly commonly develops and can become massive. Abdominal symptoms develop from the mass effect, and intermittent infarction. Both are alleviated by splenectomy. Some patients with CLL may develop an autoimmune hemolytic anemia that is resistant to standard chemotherapy, but responds well to splenectomy. Removal of the spleen, which does not affect the cause of the leukemia, may relieve the symptoms of massive splenomegaly, decrease the need for transfusions, and facilitate further transfusions.

ANSWER 49

A, B, C & D.

ANSWER 50

E.

ANSWER 51

A & B. Squamous cell cancers account for approximately 90% of head and neck malignancies. Risk factors associated with squamous cell cancers include heavy tobacco and/or alcohol use, poor oral hygiene, ultraviolet radiation, and a variety of viruses. These cancers require an exhaustive work-up to avoid missing concomitant cancers. Panendoscopy (larynx, hypopharynx, nasopharynx, esophagus) is important to avoid missing small lesions and should be performed by someone experienced in performing these exams (indirect or direct endoscopy). CT scan provides important staging information. Chest x-ray and liver enzymes are appropriate screens for metastatic disease. However, if a solitary pulmonary nodule is found in conjunction with a head and neck SCC, this is more likely a second (lung) primary and should be biopsied prior to proceeding with treatment of the head and neck tumor. Either surgical excision or radiation therapy, but not both, is an acceptable treatment option. Both are not required because this is an early stage lesion. The specifics of treatment are location-specific. In general, surgical excision is preferred because it provides pathologic confirmation of margins. However, radiotherapy provides similar treatment success and may avoid destruction of local structures.

ANSWER 52

B.

ANSWER 53

A. The most common childhood tumor is neuroblastoma and the majority of patients present with an asymptomatic abdominal mass. These tumors are most often found to arise in the adrenal gland but can also be located in the neck, mediastinum, pelvis, or extra-adrenal sympathetic chain. A tumor that is entirely confined to the site of origin is classified as stage I and is associated with a 100% survival rate if it is completely excised. Radiotherapy should be used postoperatively only when incomplete excision has been performed. Tumors that are felt to be not completely resectable, based on imaging studies, should undergo preoperative chemoradiation before proceeding with surgical resection.

Staging of Neuroblastoma

Stage	Survival with Therapy
I-Confined to site of origin	100%
IIa-Completely excised unilateral tumor, (−) nodes	80%
IIb-Unilateral tumor, (+) nodes	70%
III-Tumor across midline or contralateral (+) nodes	40%
IV-Distant metastasis	15%

ANSWER 54

C.

ANSWER 55

D.

ANSWER 56

E. This patient presents with a partial small bowel obstruction. In the setting of a previous laparotomy, the most likely cause of this obstruction (in the United States) is adhesive disease. Less common causes of small bowel obstruction include hernia, neoplasm, intussusception, volvulus, gallstone ileus, foreign bodies, strictures, and inflammatory bowel disease. Nonoperative management with nasogastric decompression and rehydration is successful in 85–90% of patients. The four cardinal signs indicating the need for prompt operative intervention are persistent focal tenderness, fever, leukocytosis, and tachycardia. These are harbingers of potentially threatened bowel. This patient will require follow-up to rule out recurrent cancer (colonoscopy and/or CT scan); however, this does not need to be done urgently.

Patients with complete bowel obstruction require immediate laparotomy. Indications of complete obstruction include, obstipation (complete cessation of flatus and stool) and lack of distal air on abdominal films.

ANSWER 57

A.

ANSWER 58

D. This patient's syndrome is consistent with another episode of biliary colic or symptomatic cholelithiasis. Cholecystitis is characterized by fever, leukocytosis, right upper quadrant pain and tenderness. In one-third of cases, a palpable mass is present. Choledocholithiasis (stone in the common bile duct) is characterized by a direct hyperbilirubinemia and biliary pain. Cholangitis is due to bacteria entering the bloodstream (*E. coli, Klebsiella, Pseudomonas, Enterococcus*) secondary to biliary obstruction. This disease is initially marked by fever, biliary colic, and jaundice (Charcot's triad). In its later stages, all of the previous signs and symptoms as well as hypotension and mental status changes (Reynold's pentad) are present. Cholangitis can be rapidly fatal and warrants emergency decompression of the bile duct (surgically or endoscopically), broad-spectrum antibiotics, and volume resuscitation.

The test of choice to document acute cholecystitis is an HIDA scan. In the presence of a stone obstructing the cystic duct, the labeled, intravenously administered iminodiacetic acid can't pass into the gallbladder. This is pathognomonic for acute cholecystitis. One might start the work-up in a new patient with abdominal ultrasound to document stones. However, this has already been done in this patient. Cholecystitis is suggested on ultrasound by pericholecystic fluid, tenderness of the gallbladder while visualizing under ultrasound, and a thickened gallbladder wall. However, these signs are not as reliable as HIDA scan.

ANSWER 59

D.

ANSWER 60

B.

ANSWER 61

D. This patient most likely has an indirect inguinal hernia. Although it is difficult to distinguish direct from indirect hernias on physical exam, in general, a hernia that extends into the scrotum is most likely an indirect hernia. The anatomy of the inguinal canal and Hesselbach's triangle helps define direct from indirect hernias. Hesselbach's triangle is formed by the inguinal ligament laterally, the rectus sheath medially, and the inferior epigastric vessels superiorly. A direct hernia protrudes through the floor of the inguinal canal within the triangle, medial to the inferior epigastric vessels. An indirect hernia forms lateral to the inferior epigastric vessels and lies within the spermatic cord and passes through the internal ring. A pantaloon hernia is one where there is both a direct and indirect component. A hernia is incarcerated if it is not reducible and is strangulated when the irreducible contents have a compromised blood supply. The current preferred procedure for an inguinal hernia is a tension-free mesh repair. The classic repairs use permanent suture to reinforce the internal inguinal ring and the floor of the inguinal canal, and do not use mesh. Examples of these include the Marcy, Bassini, Shouldice, and McVay repairs. A Lichtenstein procedure uses mesh which helps achieve a tension-free repair. There are many different variations of the Lichtenstein repair. A Stoppa procedure is an open approach where a giant piece of mesh is placed preperitoneally. Complications vary by the type of repair and the surgeons' experience, but generally range from 7% to 12%. The reported recurrence rate for groin hernias is anywhere from less than 1% to 10%. Other complications include: hematomas, hydroceles, parasthesias, chronic pain, seromas, and testicular ischemia. Some patients have difficulty voiding immediately after repair, but there are usually no long-term urinary tract problems.

ANSWER 62

C. Ninety percent of bladder cancers are transitional cell tumors, with the remainder being either squamous cell or adenocarcinoma. Men are affected three times more frequently than women. The risk of developing bladder cancer is increased by smoking and exposure to beta-naphthylamine and/or paraminodiphenyl. Most patients present with hematuria. Frequent UTIs, bladder irritability with frequency and dysuria are common. Urinary cytology may reveal bladder cancer and excretory urography may demonstrate the lesion. Cystoscopy with biopsy should be performed to confirm the diagnosis. Treatment for local disease is usually transurethral resection followed by chemotherapy while locally advanced disease is treated with radical cystectomy with radiation and chemotherapy.

BLOCK **THREE**

ANSWERS

ANSWER 63

A.

ANSWER 64

A. Nonselective shunts are technically less challenging than selective shunts (distal splenorenal/Warren shunt). The Warren shunt requires a patent splenic vein that is at least 7 mm in diameter, to be technically feasible. Nonselective shunts typically have a lower rate of failure although they do not offer a survival benefit over selective shunts. There is a higher rate of postoperative encephalopathy after nonselective shunts. The distal splenorenal shunt diverts blood flow away from varices while preserving hepatic flow, therefore accounting for the decreased incidence of encephalopathy. The amount of shunt surgery performed in the United States has decreased markedly over the past 10–15 years as a result of the success of sclerotherapy, variceal banding, and transjugular intrahepatic portosystemic shunts (TIPSS). TIPSS is very successful for decompressing varices and preventing recurrent bleeding. Its main drawback is a relatively high rate of stenosis of the stent. Therefore, for a patient in whom relatively frequent follow-up is not possible (remote location), it is advisable to perform a more durable (surgical) variceal procedure.

ANSWER 65

B. The patient is a Childs B. This scale was specifically developed to estimate operative mortality for cirrhotics undergoing shunt surgery.

Childs Class (points)	1	2	3
Ascites	Absent	Slight	Tense
Encephalopathy	None	Grades 1 & II	Grades III & IV
Albumin	>3.5	3.0–3.5	<3.0
Bilirubin	<2.0	2.0–3.0	>3.0
PT (seconds above normal)	<4.0	4.0–6.0	>6.0

Class A: 5–6 points (1% mortality), Class B: 7–9 points (10% mortality), Class C: 10–15 points (50% mortality)

ANSWER 66

A.

ANSWER 67

D. You have tried the standard measures for cardiopulmonary bypass weaning in this high-risk patient. Intra-aortic balloon counter pulsation is an effective means for dealing with this situation. This device decreases afterload by deflating during systole, therefore decreasing the amount of resistance against which the left ventricle must pump. The balloon inflates during diastole, increasing aortic pressure, which augments coronary and visceral perfusion. It is better to make the decision to place a balloon pump quickly, rather than let the heart struggle; therefore, in this scenario further inotropic management is not ideal. Trial of a balloon pump is indicated prior to placing assist devices. In addition, assist devices outside of clinical trials are used as a bridge to transplantation, and this elderly diabetic patient is not a candidate for transplantation and should therefore probably not be considered for an assist device. You obtained a complete revascularization and have no evidence that ischemia is the reason the patient cannot be weaned from bypass, therefore placement of another graft is not recommended. Aortic insufficiency is an absolute contraindication to placement of an intra-aortic balloon pump. With an incompetent aortic valve, a balloon pump worsens the aortic regurgitation and compromises hemodynamic status.

ANSWER 68

C. This patient has a postoperative wound infection. Therapy for this problem consists of opening and packing the wound. Antibiotic therapy without opening the wound is inappropriate. Antibiotic use in addition to opening the wound is superfluous.

ANSWER 69

C.

ANSWER 70

C.

ANSWER 71

D. This patient presents with acute pseudo-obstruction (Ogilvie's syndrome), a paralytic ileus of the large intestine. Painless distention is a common presenting finding. Risk factors include severe blunt trauma, orthopedic trauma or procedures, cardiac disease, acute neurologic disease, and acute metabolic derangements. The condition is quite dangerous due to increasing distention of the cecum that can perforate when its diameter expands beyond 10–12 cm. Observation while correcting metabolic derangements and minimizing narcotics is acceptable initially, but when the cecum becomes distended to the point shown in the abdominal film, immediate decompression is necessary. Decompression can be achieved with colonoscopy or neostigmine with the current trend being toward neostigmine administration if there are no contraindications. Correction of electrolytes and metabolic derangements are critical in this management. Cecostomy, cecopexy, and hemicolectomy have been utilized in the past to prevent recurrences. However, the efficacy of these procedures has not been proven. Surgical intervention is usually only necessary if perforation occurs. Right hemicolectomy is the standard surgical procedure when this morbid complication occurs.

BLOCK **FOUR**

ANSWERS

ANSWER 72

C. This patient's presentation is concerning for ruptured abdominal aortic aneurysm. You will quickly and simultaneously perform a number of tasks to rule in or out this diagnosis. The first priority is to alert the operating room team to allow them time to prepare. You will also establish IV access, begin fluid resuscitation, send appropriate labs, and obtain a brief but detailed medical and surgical history. A CT scan is very helpful for confirming the diagnosis of abdominal aortic aneurysm. However, this patient is hemodynamically unstable and is not a candidate for a trip to radiology. An aortogram is inappropriate for the same reasons. Lower extremity duplex is not relevant for this problem. If the patient is hemodynamically unstable and the history and exam suggest ruptured aneurysm, you should proceed directly to the operating room for exploration.

ANSWER 73

B. The most common cause of hemodynamically significant, lower GI bleeding is angiodysplasia or AVM. The second most common cause is a bleeding diverticulum. This occurs when a diverticulum erodes into a penetrating artery causing significant bleeding. Colon cancer typically causes occult GI bleeding rather than acute blood loss. Patients typically present with iron deficiency anemia. Likewise, diverticulitis does not typically cause acute blood loss. Overall, the most common source of lower GI bleeding (bright red blood per rectum) is an upper GI bleed with rapid transit. In this case, however, the likelihood of an upper GI source is very small, because the NG aspirate revealed bile without blood, essentially eliminating the stomach and duodenum from consideration as the source of the bleeding.

ANSWER 74

A. While there is much disagreement over the relative merits of various techniques to determine the presence and location of ongoing bleeding, the most sensitive technique is a tagged red blood cell scan. This test can document 0.1–0.5 cc/min of blood loss. The procedure involves withdrawing the patient's blood, labeling it with technetium-99, and reinfusing, after which the patient is scanned at numerous intervals. This test can document bleeding and potentially localize it to the left or right colon. However, the results can be obscured by the overlying small bowel. It also does not afford a therapeutic option and the patient must spend a significant amount of time in the radiology department, possibly without monitoring, which can be dangerous in the setting of an acute GI bleed. Colonoscopy is, in most centers, the first diagnostic option. It offers the opportunity to definitively treat a bleeding source once it is located. It is well tolerated and can be performed in the ICU. The ultimate success of the procedure is dependent upon a satisfactory bowel prep. Angiography also offers an opportunity for definitive treatment with embolization of the arteries that are bleeding. This last choice is particularly attractive in the elderly patient with multiple comorbidities who may not be a satisfactory operative candidate. There is potential, however, for bowel ischemia and infarction after this procedure. Angiography can document bleeding if the rate is at least 1 cc/min.

ANSWER 75

D. Perirectal abscess in an immunocompromised patient must be widely incised and drained, which can be adequately accomplished only in the operating room. Parenteral antibiotics are warranted. An insufficiently drained abscess in the immunocompromised patient can quickly become a devastating perineal soft tissue infection. In the immunocompetent patient this can often be accomplished with local anesthesia. If symptoms return, one must suspect a more complicated ischiorectal abscess or an underlying fistula.

ANSWER 76

E. In 50% cases of documented AFHF, the inciting event is never determined. Hepatitis A accounts for approximately 5% of cases, hepatitis B 15%, acetaminophen and other toxins 33%, and hepatitis C 0%.

ANSWER 77

E. A wide constellation of clinical findings accompanies fulminant hepatic failure. The mainstay of therapy is to support all of the physiologic systems of the body to allow the liver time to regenerate or to allow sufficient time for a suitable donor liver to be identified. Frequent abnormalities include abnormal coagulation, electrolyte and acid base imbalances, hypoglycemia, hypertension or hypotension, cerebral edema and elevated intracranial pressure, acute renal failure, and cardiac arrhythmias.

ANSWER 78

B. In an older man with a recent history of diverticulitis, the most likely etiology of this lesion is a bacterial (pyogenic) abscess. Pyogenic abscesses typically are secondary to one of a number of sources: (1) portal vein bacteremia from diverticulitis or appendicitis, (2) biliary obstruction (benign or malignant) and cholangitis, (3) hepatic artery bacteremia from endocarditis, (4) direct extension from gangrenous cholecystitis or subhepatic abscess, (5) superinfection of necrosing malignancy, or (6) necrosis from hepatic trauma.

ANSWER 79

C. Left untreated, pyogenic liver abscess is uniformly fatal. Initial therapy for pyogenic abscess is broad-spectrum antibiotics and CT guided percutaneous drainage. This is successful in approximately 80% of cases. Indications for surgical drainage include the necessity for laparotomy for the underlying disorder, such as a diverticular abscess. IV antibiotics alone have been used successfully in some patients; however, results vary widely and this is not the standard of care. Antibiotics alone might be used for a patient with multiple, widely distributed, small abscesses.

ANSWER 80

B. This clinical scenario is characteristic of a patient with an amebic abscess of the liver, caused by the organism *Entameba Histolytica*. This typically occurs in young men who have emigrated from or those who have recently traveled to an endemic area. Symptoms are nonspecific but most often include pain, fever, and anorexia. Diagnosis is secured by the indirect hemagglutination test with titers greater than 1:512. This ratio is characteristic of invasive disease and a ratio of at least 1:128 is suggestive of liver abscess. Initial therapy is oral metronidazole, which cures 75% of patients with amebic disease of the liver. Drainage is reserved for patients who fail initial therapy. Ampicillin, gentamicin, and metronidazole would be an appropriate antibiotic choice for pyogenic liver abscess, which typically contains gram-negative bacteria and anaerobes.

ANSWER 81

A. This patient is in shock, likely from intra-abdominal hemorrhage. The patient has not responded to an adequate trial of crystalloid infusion and therefore the next appropriate step in management is to transfuse blood. Because the patient just arrived, type specific or cross-matched blood will not be available. Therefore, O-negative (trauma) blood is appropriate. A hemodynamically unstable patient should not be taken to the radiology suite. Chest x-ray is an important component of the evaluation of a trauma patient. However, you have assessed this patient with the "primary survey" and found him to be in shock. You must therefore address this problem as your first priority.

ANSWER 82

A. The radial nerve is closely associated to the distal humerus in the radial groove. Approximately 10% of humeral fractures have an associated radial nerve injury. These are often the result of stretching or contusion of the nerve and most recover with nonoperative management. In addition, the results of delayed operative repair for complete injuries are comparable to those for immediate repair. Therefore, an appropriate course of action is expectant management followed by operative intervention if necessary.

ANSWER 83

C.

ANSWER 84

C. Traumatic aortic disruption is a highly morbid injury with at least 85% of patients dying at the accident scene. Additionally, there is a 50% in-hospital mortality for every 24 hr that the injury goes undiagnosed. Therefore, it is critical to have a high index of suspicion. The chest radiograph demonstrates several non-specific findings suggestive of aortic injury.

The gold standard for diagnosing aortic injury remains aortography. However, modalities such as contrast enhanced spiral CT scan and transesophageal echocardiography are gaining acceptance and have been used to screen for this injury. The vast majority (90–95%) of patients who arrive at the hospital alive have an injury at the isthmus just proximal to the left subclavian takeoff. Standard treatment is the surgical placement of an aortic interposition graft.

ANSWER 85

C.

ANSWER 86

A.

ANSWER 87

B.

ANSWER 88

A. The patient in the above scenario has carcinoid syndrome that classically presents with flushing (95%), diarrhea (80%), valvular heart disease (40%), and wheezing (20%). Carcinoid tumors secrete serotonin, the hormone responsible for the syndrome. The systemic effects of carcinoid syndrome do not present until metastatic disease occurs in the liver. This is because the liver "filters" or metabolizes the serotonin. With metastases, some active serotonin passes directly into the central circulation, accounting for the syndrome. In general, appendiceal carcinoid tumors are not as aggressive as carcinoid tumors in the ileum (the second most common place for carcinoids). However, tumor size greater than 2 cm is associated with a 90% risk of metastases. The classic lab test to diagnose carcinoid syndrome is the serum serotonin or a 24-hr urinary 5-hydroxyindoleacetic acid (5-HIAA) level. Unfortunately, carcinoid tumors have minimal clinical manifestations until metastases occur. Carcinoid tumors are usually found incidentally at appendectomy. Treatment for carcinoid depends on tumor location and size. For appendiceal carcinoids, tumors of less than 2 cm require appendectomy only. For tumors greater than 2 cm, right hemicolectomy is advocated. Small bowel carcinoids require wide en bloc resection including nodal drainage. Treatment of metastatic disease usually consists of treatment of the carcinoid syndrome. Surgical resection does not prolong survival with metastatic disease. Octreotide and alpha interferon have shown promise in alleviating symptoms. Chemotherapy is only marginally effective.

ANSWER 89

D.

ANSWER 90

C. This patient has two possible diagnoses, infection and testicular torsion. Testicular torsion is an emergency because complete strangulation of the blood supply renders the testicle surgically unsalvageable after about 6 hr. All of the tests listed should be done to rule out infection and to evaluate the blood supply to the testicle. Torsion is usually seen in young males who present complaining of the rapid onset of severe testicular pain followed by testicular swelling. Physical exam may reveal a high riding, swollen, tender testicle, oriented horizontally in the scrotum. Doppler ultrasound should be obtained to evaluate blood flow in the testicle. Once the diagnosis is confirmed or if the diagnosis is unclear, surgical exploration should be performed. Orchiopexy is required to save the testicle and because the deformity is usually bilateral, orchiopexy of the contralateral testicle should also be done at the same time.

ANSWER 91

A.

ANSWER 92

C. In all traumas the ABCs (A = airway, B = breathing, C = circulation) are your first priority. To evaluate the airway in an intubated patient, you should check an end-tidal carbon dioxide, which can quickly and easily be done in the emergency department. Next you should evaluate breathing in your patient. Breath sounds are difficult to hear in the trauma bay but should be checked and at the same time palpate the chest to evaluate for rib fractures, crepitance and/or flail chest. The next step is to evaluate circulation by evaluating perfusion of the extremities and palpating pulses. IV access should be obtained with two large bore antecubital IVs. With continued unstable vital signs and the presence of multiple rib fractures, you should be worried about a tension pneumothorax, which can easily be treated in the emergency department with needle decompression and tube thoracostomy. A chest x-ray will take too long to process and an unstable patient with a tension pneumothorax could be dead by the time the chest x-ray is obtained. If the patient does not respond to this treatment, you should begin to think of other causes of hypotension including hemorrhagic shock. An unstable patient should not be taken to the radiology department for an extended procedure.

ANSWER 93

B. Gastric ulcer formation involves a compromised mucosal surface undergoing acid-peptic digestion. Factors that alter mucosal defenses include nonsteroidal anti-inflammatory drugs, alcohol, tobacco use, and *Helicobacter pylori* infection. Surgical treatment of gastric ulcers in the acute setting is indicated for perforation or massive bleeding. Malignant gastric ulcers are indistinguishable from benign ulcers. Therefore, the operation for gastric ulcers should always include excisional biopsy of the ulcer to rule out malignancy. Surgical treatment then involves wedge resection of the ulcer if the lesion is benign.

ANSWER 94

C.

ANSWER 95

A.

ANSWER 96

C. Patients with stone disease usually present with acute onset of pain in the flank that radiates to the groin. The patient is often unable to find a comfortable position, and vomiting is common. Dysuria, frequency and hematuria may be present. Stones are most commonly calcium phosphate and calcium oxalate (80%), struvite (15%), uric acid (5%), and cystine (1%). Calcium stones and struvite stones are more common in women. Uric acid stones are twice as common in men. Cystine stones occur in men and women with the same frequency. Evaluation of the urine will reveal hematuria unless the affected ureter is totally obstructed. An abdominal x-ray may be helpful since calcium, struvite, and cystine stones are all radio-opaque. Intravenous pyelogram allows diagnosis of stones by outlining defects in the ureter or identifying complete obstruction. Retrograde pyelogram is useful for assessing the degree and level of obstruction. Most commonly a CT scan without contrast is used to evaluate for stones.

ANSWER 97A

C.

ANSWER 97B

C.

ANSWER 98

B.

ANSWER 99

 A.

ANSWER 100A

 C.

ANSWER 100B

A. The most common cause of small bowel obstruction in the United States is adhesions. Colorectal surgery, gynecological surgery, hernia repair, and appendectomy are the most common surgeries that predispose patients to adhesion formation. Recent large retrospective analyses document a recurrence rate for repeated obstruction between 35% and 50%, but the strongest predictor of future obstruction is the number of previous admissions for small bowel obstruction. In this patient, there is no previous surgical history to suggest his obstruction is due to adhesions; therefore, immediate operative management is indicated due to the high probability of malignancy or internal hernia. There is no diagnostic test that should keep the surgeon out of the operating room in this situation, and obtaining an unnecessary test can only blur the clinical picture and delay appropriate therapy. A period of observation for spontaneous resolution of obstruction is acceptable in patients with a history of previous abdominal surgery, stable clinical picture, and with an obstruction most likely due to adhesions. Abdominal CT scan or enteroclysis can be used to investigate the obstruction. The treatment modality of colonoscopy has no role in the management of small bowel obstruction. Sonography has been used in Japan with some frequency, but is not employed commonly in the United States. The abdominal films show multiple air-fluid levels and dilated loops of small bowel. Sentinal loops can only be confirmed after multiple abdominal films showing no change in the single visualized loop.